DEADLY CREATURES
DICTIONARY

An A to Z of dangerous animals

Author Clint Twist
Editor Elise See Tai
Art Editor Julia Harris
Art Director Miranda Kennedy
Cover Designer Arvind Shah
Production Director Clive Sparling
Consultant Zoologist Valerie Davies
Illustrators Richard Bonson (The Art Agency), Robin Bouttell
(The Art Agency), Myke Taylor (The Art Agency), Gill Tomblin.
Andromeda Children's Books would like to apologise in advance
for any unintentional omissions.

Created and produced by
Andromeda Children's Books
An imprint of Alligator Books Ltd
Gadd House
Arcadia Avenue
London N3 2JU
UK

This edition produced in 2007 for Scholastic Inc.
Published by Tangerine Press, an imprint of Scholastic Inc.,
557 Broadway, New York, NY 10012

Scholastic and Tangerine Press and associated logos are trademarks
of Scholastic Inc.

ISBN-10: 0-545-02803-5
ISBN-13: 978-0-545-02803-5

Printed in Malaysia

Information icons

Throughout this dictionary, there are special icons
next to each entry. These give you more information
about each creature.

Globes

These show you where each creature can be found
in the world. Small red dots on the globes clearly
show the locations.

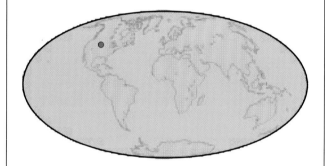

Size comparison pictures

Next to each entry you will see a symbol, either
a hand or an adult human next to a red icon of
the creature listed. The symbol shows you the
size of each creature in real life compared to
the size of a human.

18 centimetres

The first symbol is a human
adult's hand, which measures about
18 centimetres (7 inches) from the
wrist to the tip of the longest
finger. Some creatures are smaller
than this, so this symbol helps you
to imagine their size.

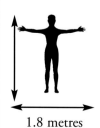

1.8 metres

The second symbol is an adult
human. The height of the human
is about 1.8 metres (6 feet). With
arms outstretched, the arm span
also measures about 1.8 metres
(6 feet). This symbol helps you to
compare the height or length of a
creature to a human.

DEADLY CREATURES DICTIONARY

An A to Z of dangerous animals

tangerine Press®

an imprint of

SCHOLASTIC

www.scholastic.com

Animal killers

All the animals in this book are natural-born killers – killing other animals is their way of life – and they are very good at what they do. Most of these deadly creatures are deliberate killers. They are either predators, such as panthers and crocodiles, that eat other animals, or they are prey with highly-effective defence weapons. Some deadly creatures, however, are accidental killers. They kill neither for food nor to defend themselves – they just happen to have a way of life that is deadly to certain other animals.

Panther

Osprey

Feeding habits

Animals that eat other animals are usually described as carnivores (meat eaters), while those that eat leaves, stems and fruit are described as herbivores (plant eaters). Mammals and birds that eat small prey, such as insects, are sometimes described as insectivores, even though they also eat snails, slugs and worms. Predators and prey are linked by food chains that end with top predators. The food chains in a particular place are linked together in a food web.

Estuarine
crocodile

Self-defence

Running away or hiding are often the best ways
for prey to avoid being eaten by predators, but
there are some interesting alternatives. Some of the world's most dangerous creatures
are prey and are prey animals that have deadly defence weapons. Not all these
animals are herbivores. Some are also predators in their
own right that can defend themselves with teeth and
claws. Even small, seemingly harmless animals, such
as the poison dart frog, may have deadly secrets.

Flea

Parasites

Parasites are animals that attach themselves
to and feed on the living body of another animal,
which is known as a host. Some parasites invade the
body and attach themselves to internal organs, while
others remain outside, attached to the skin. Parasites do not
intentionally kill their hosts, because that
would deprive them of food. Some skin
parasites change host frequently, and in
doing so, they can transmit deadly disease
from one host to another.

Ichneumon
wasp

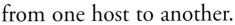

How predators attack

Predators hunt and attack their prey. Some animals hunt alone, while others hunt in groups. All of them have special strengths, senses and features to help them attack and catch their prey.

Killer features

Grizzly bear

Many predators have jaws that serve two purposes – they are used for both killing and eating. Sharks rotate their bodies when they bite so that their razor-sharp teeth cut away huge chunks of flesh. A single bite from a great white shark is enough to kill all but the largest marine animals. Barracuda and piranha take smaller bites, but they usually attack in such large numbers that they quickly kill their prey.

On land, predators often strike at the vulnerable neck area. Wolverines kill deer and caribou by biting through the neck, while wolves and wild dogs often kill small prey by shaking the animal until its neck breaks. Big cats often use their jaws to clamp their victim's mouth closed so that it cannot breathe. Grizzly bears usually kill by slicing open their prey's belly with their long, sharp claws.

Ethiopian wolf

Poisonous substances

Great white shark

Venom is a substance produced by an animal for the purpose of killing another animal. Most venoms are fairly similar – they quickly spread through the blood and attack nerves and muscles. The differences are in the way that they are delivered.

Venomous snakes have long, sharp fangs that pierce their victim's skin and allow the venom to enter the body. Some snakes have hollow fangs that work like hypodermic syringes. Spiders also deliver their venom through fangs, while scorpions carry their venomous sting in their tails. Venomous fish usually deliver their poison through needle-like spines.

There are also many other causes of death in the world of deadly creatures. Some animals, such as the electric eel, use electricity, some carry fatal diseases, while others eat their victims from the inside out!

Red spitting cobra

Electric eel

Aardwolf

Max length: 95 cm (37½ in)

The aardwolf lives in the scrublands of eastern and southern Africa. These are the areas of land covered with stunted trees or shrubs. The aardwolf hides in a burrow during the day and comes out at night to search for food. It is related to hyenas, but unlike its relatives, it does not hunt large prey. This unusual animal is a mass killer – of insects. It feeds mainly on termites and can eat more than 200,000 in a single night, using its long, sticky tongue to collect them.

African hunting dog

Max length: 1.5 m (5 ft)

This rare animal is one of the most aggressive and persistent hunters on the African grasslands. It lives and hunts in packs that can have as many as 50 members. The pack works together to track and bring down large prey, such as wildebeest and zebra. After a successful hunt, the whole pack shares in the feast of fresh meat.

Max length: 5 m (16½ ft)

Alligator, American

This alligator is a large, powerful reptile with about 80 sharp teeth. It is found in the southeastern US. It lives in swamps and lakes, where it often floats with only its eyes and nostrils showing above the water's surface. The alligator feeds mainly on fish, but it can jump several feet out of the water to seize birds and small mammals from overhanging branches.

Anaconda

The anaconda is the heaviest snake in the world and may weigh more than 250 kilograms (550 lb). It is found near rivers in the rainforests of South America, and spends most of its time in the water. The anaconda will attack animal prey larger than a human being. It winds its powerful body around its prey and slowly squeezes its victim to death before swallowing the animal whole.

Max length: 9 m (29½ ft)

Angelshark, Pacific

Max length: 1.5 m (5 ft)

The Pacific angelshark is a very lazy predator. It lives in shallow water and spends most of its time half-buried in the sandy seabed, where it is almost invisible. When a fish or squid swims within range, the angelshark opens its wide mouth, which is lined with sharp teeth. It then seizes its prey with astonishing speed.

Aa

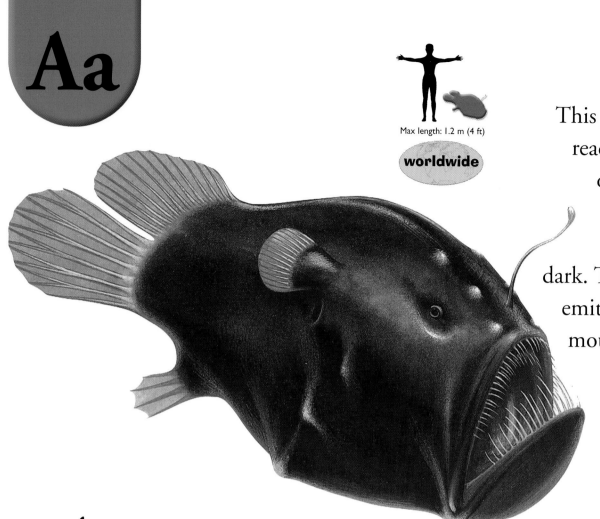

Max length: 1.2 m (4 ft)

worldwide

Anglerfish

This predator lives beyond the reach of sunlight in the deep oceans, where many small animals, such as shrimps and jellyfish, glow in the dark. The anglerfish has a light-emitting organ above its huge mouth. Any hungry fish that come to investigate the light are quickly seized and swallowed.

Max length: 2 cm (¾ in)

Army ant

The army ant is found in South and Central America, and also in Africa, where it is called a driver ant. Army ants live in colonies of up to 20 million insects, but they do not have a permanent home. Instead, they are constantly on the move. They march through rainforests in columns that are about 10 metres (33 ft) wide and eat everything in their path.

Fact
Most of the army ants in a colony are completely blind. They find their way by following scent trails left by the scout ants that can see.

Max length: 2 m (6½ ft)

worldwide

Barracuda

The barracuda is a large, fast-swimming predator that lives in warm, tropical waters. It feeds mainly on other fish. The barracuda often hunts in groups of about a dozen barracudas – they are sometimes called the wolves of the sea. Unlike real wolves, these fish do not cooperate with each other while hunting.

Max length: 28 cm (11 in)

Bird-eating spider

The goliath bird-eating spider lives in northern South America. It is one of the few spiders large enough to hunt small birds and mammals. It does not spin a web to catch its prey. Instead, it prowls along tree branches at night, and sinks its fangs into its victims while they are asleep.

Bb

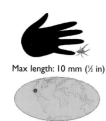

Max length: 10 mm (½ in)

Black widow

This small spider has a fearsome reputation. All spiders use venom to kill their prey, but the black widow is one of the few that can kill a human being with a single bite. Only the female is dangerous – it is 15 times more poisonous than a rattlesnake. Black widows are found in many warm regions of the world, including the southern US. These deadly spiders spin small, scrappy webs, often in the corners of unoccupied buildings, and even under furniture.

Fact
The black widow spider has a distinctive hourglass-shaped red marking on the underside of its glossy black abdomen.

Max length: 4.6 m (15 ft)

worldwide

Bluefin tuna

The bluefin tuna is one of the ocean's most efficient predators. This huge, powerful fish patrols the surface waters in large packs or shoals in search of smaller fish, such as mackerel. When bluefins attack a shoal of mackerel, they accelerate to high speed and can change direction very quickly when chasing their smaller prey.

Bull shark

Max length: 3.5 m (11½ ft)

worldwide

This heavy-bodied shark is often seen in coastal waters, and also in some freshwater rivers and lakes. One bull shark was spotted in the Mississippi River more than 1,600 kilometres (994 miles) from the sea. The bull shark will eat just about anything that moves and is believed to be responsible for many of the reported shark attacks on human beings.

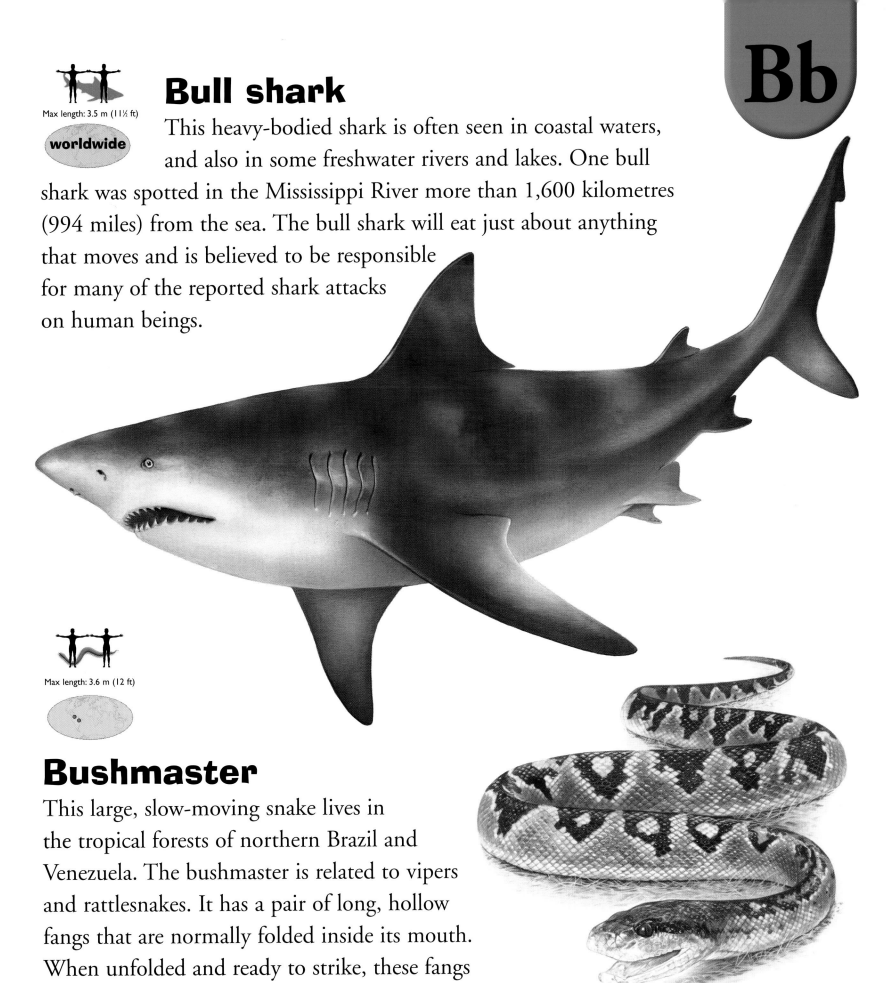

Max length: 3.6 m (12 ft)

Bushmaster

This large, slow-moving snake lives in the tropical forests of northern Brazil and Venezuela. The bushmaster is related to vipers and rattlesnakes. It has a pair of long, hollow fangs that are normally folded inside its mouth. When unfolded and ready to strike, these fangs can deliver a large amount of deadly venom.

Cc

Max length: 6 m (19¾ ft)

Caiman, black

The black caiman is the biggest of the South American crocodiles and is usually greenish-brown rather than black. It lives in rivers and mainly feeds on fish and other water creatures. The black caiman is strong enough to bring down large mammals, such as tapirs, that approach the river's edge for a drink.

Max length: 1.5 m (5 ft)

Cheetah

This cat is the world's fastest land animal – it can reach speeds of 100 km/h (60 mph) in short bursts. The cheetah uses its incredible speed to chase down prey on the grasslands of East Africa. It sinks its curved claws into its fleeing victim's flesh and drags the animal down onto the ground.

Civet

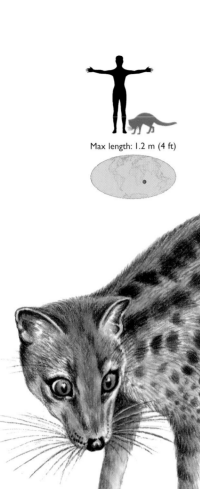

Max length: 1.2 m (4 ft)

The civet lives in the tropical forests of Madagascar. It sometimes feeds on fruit and flowers, but it also hunts insects, small mammals, and birds and their eggs. Civets, along with mongooses and genets, are more closely related to cats than they are to either dogs or stoats and weasels.

Fact

The legless cobra 'walks' along the ground on its ribs, which are attached to the wide scales on the underside of its body.

Cobra, Indian

Max length: 2.1 m (7 ft)

The Indian cobra is one of the world's most dangerous snakes. When threatened, it raises its head off the ground and widens its neck into a distinctive hood. From this position, the Indian cobra can strike forwards with astonishing speed to deliver a dose of deadly venom from its long front fangs.

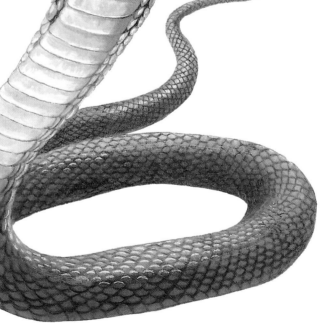

Cc

Max length: 3.5 cm (1⅓ in)

worldwide

Cockroach, German

This medium-sized insect is not a deliberate killer. The German cockroach, like other cockroaches, feeds on decaying plants or animals that are already dead. This particular cockroach has discovered a new habitat in human homes and other buildings. It leaves a trail of droppings wherever it walks. These droppings on food can spread many dangerous diseases. Despite its name, it is originally from Africa and has now spread to almost every part of the world.

Max length: 20 cm (8 in)

Cone shell

The cone shell is a predatory marine snail that hunts other molluscs. It is found in the Indian and Pacific oceans. Inside its shell, the animal has a sharp sting that can shoot out and inject deadly venom into its victim. Some cone shells have venom that is strong enough to kill a human being in a matter of minutes.

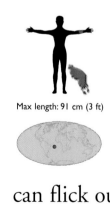

Max length: 91 cm (3 ft)

Cuttlefish, giant

The giant cuttlefish is a superbly-designed killer. This mollusc has large eyes to find prey and two special hunting tentacles that can flick out at high speed to capture food. A cuttlefish is special because it can make its skin pulse with coloured patterns to dazzle and confuse its prey.

Darter, Indian

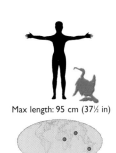

Max length: 95 cm (37½ in)

The Indian darter can be seen throughout most of Africa, southern Asia and parts of Australia. This waterbird is a highly-efficient predator. It swims with its body underwater and only its head and neck above the surface. The darter catches fish by spearing them with its sharp, pointed beak.

Fact

The darter is also known as the snake bird, as its head and neck resemble the body of a snake when its body is under the water.

Diving beetle, great

Max length: 5 cm (2 in)

worldwide

This air-breathing insect is a deadly underwater killer. The great diving beetle traps bubbles of air beneath its wing cases, then dives below the surface in search of prey. An adult beetle will attack fish that are several times longer than itself. It grabs its prey with its front legs so that its jaws can deliver a killing bite.

Dd

Dolphin, spinner

Max length: 2.4 m (8 ft)

worldwide

The long-snouted spinner dolphin is one of the most widespread of all the dolphins. Although the dolphin can appear playful in captivity, it is a fierce and intelligent hunter in the wild. This marine mammal hunts in packs. They use sound echoes to find their prey and use other sounds to communicate with each other. Dolphins attack large prey, such as other dolphins, by ramming them at high speed.

Fact
There are approximately 31 species of dolphins – 26 species of oceanic dolphins and 5 species of river dolphins.

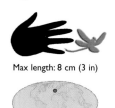

Max length: 8 cm (3 in)

Dragonfly, brown hawker

The brown hawker dragonfly is a superb hunter at all stages of its life. The dragonfly larvae hatch from eggs underwater and feed on small animals, such as tadpoles. When fully grown, the larvae rise to the surface and change into flying insects. Adult dragonflies have excellent eyesight so that they can find and chase mosquitoes in midair.

Larva

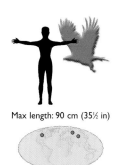

Eagle, golden

Max length: 90 cm (35½ in)

The golden eagle is a large bird of prey that is found throughout North America, Europe and northern Asia. It has a wingspan of more than 2 metres (6½ ft) and spends much of its time soaring on air currents. An eagle can spot prey, such as a rabbit, from a distance of about 5 kilometres (3 miles). It then strikes without warning, swooping down to seize its victim in its strong talons.

Electric eel

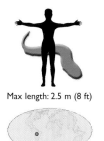

Max length: 2.5 m (8 ft)

This unusual fish lives in the rivers of South America. It has an eel-like body but is not a true eel. Like some marine rays, this fish has the ability to generate and store electricity in its muscles. A fully-grown electric eel can deliver an electric shock of about 600 volts, which is enough to stun or kill a large animal or a human being.

Ee

Max length: 8.5 m (28 ft)

Estuarine crocodile

The estuarine crocodile, which is also known as the saltwater crocodile, lives around the coasts of tropical Australasia and parts of Southeast Asia. It is the largest and most dangerous of all the crocodiles and alligators and is responsible for several attacks on humans each year. It has also been known to attack small boats.

Max length: 1.3 m (4¼ ft)

Ethiopian wolf

The Ethiopian wolf is also sometimes known as the Simien jackal. It is found only in a few remote parts of the Ethiopian mountains in Africa. These wolves live in family groups of about a dozen adults and youngsters. The adults hunt hares and other small mammals.

Fennec fox

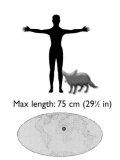

Max length: 75 cm (29½ in)

The fennec fox is the smallest of all the foxes. It lives in the Sahara Desert of North Africa and stays in its burrow during the heat of the day. After dark, the fennec fox emerges to search for food. It has sharp claws and teeth and sometimes hunts small mammals using its large ears to detect the faint sounds of movement in the quiet of the desert night.

Fact

Some 650 years ago, rat fleas spread a disease known as the Black Death, which killed about one in every three people in Europe.

Flea

Max length: 3 mm (⅒ in)

worldwide

This small, wingless insect is one of the world's accidental killers. It is a parasite that attaches itself to the skin of birds and mammals and uses its pointed mouthparts to suck tiny amounts of blood. When the flea moves from one animal to another, its mouthparts can transfer small traces of blood. If the blood is diseased, then the flea will spread the disease.

Ff

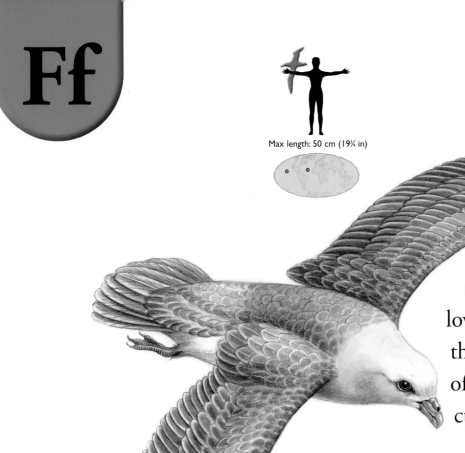

Max length: 50 cm (19¾ in)

Fulmar

The fulmar is widespread in the northern Atlantic and Pacific oceans. This seabird is a tireless hunter that spends almost all of its time in the air. It then swoops low over the sea to grab fish and squid at the surface. The fulmar is a close relative of the albatross and has the same type of curved tip to its beak, which is designed to keep hold of slippery prey.

Funnel-web spider

Max length: 4 cm (1½ in)

This deadly spider lives in woodland in southern Australia. It does not spin a proper web, but lines its burrow with a funnel-shaped tangle of silk. At night, it wanders around in search of the snails, slugs and small amphibians on which it feeds. It kills its prey by injecting venom that is strong enough to kill a human being.

Fact

Around the Australian capital city of Sydney, the funnel-web spider is often found in garages and gardens – and even underneath the floors of houses.

Max length: 50 cm (19¾ in)

Gila monster

The gila monster is a medium-sized, slow-moving lizard that lives in the deserts of the southwestern US. It feeds on small mammals, nestling birds and birds' eggs. It is poorly equipped for chasing after its prey, but is one of only two venomous lizards. The gila monster has to chew its victim to deliver venom into the animal. Although the venom is deadly to small animals, it is not usually strong enough to kill a human being.

Max length: 8 m (26 ft)

worldwide

Great white shark

The great white shark is the largest of the sharp-toothed sharks and has a fearsome reputation. It may be found around temperate coastlines in all parts of the world, but it is now quite a rare animal. The great white feeds mainly on marine mammals, such as seals and sea lions, which are killed with a single bite of its powerful jaws.

Gg

Max length: 10 cm (4 in)

Greater bulldog bat

This small bat lives in the warmer parts of South America. During the day, it sleeps in caves and hollow trees. It comes out at night to feed. Unlike most other bats, which eat either fruit or flying insects, the greater bulldog bat feeds on fish and crabs. It swoops down and grabs its prey with the strong claws on its back feet.

Fact
The largest brown bears, which are up to 3 metres (10 ft) tall, are found on Kodiak Island near the coast of Alaska.

Max height: 3.2 m (10½ ft)

Grizzly bear

The grizzly bear is one of the American names for the brown bear that lives in the coniferous forests of North America, Europe and Asia. In other places, it is known as the Siberian bear or the Hokkaido bear. Although it feeds mainly on plants and fruit, this large, powerful bear often catches fish with its sharp claws and hunts for meat.

Max length: 60 cm (23⅗ in)

Hawk, rough-legged

The rough-legged hawk is widespread across the northern parts of Europe, Asia and North America. This bird of prey hunts from a high perch, such as a tree branch. It dives to the ground to grab mice and voles with the sharp talons on its feet.

Max length: 3.2 m (10½ ft)

Hippopotamus

In terms of human deaths and injuries, this large, heavy, plant-eating mammal is by far the most dangerous animal in Africa. Although it spends most of its time in rivers, a hippopotamus will often wander about on land in search of food. If it becomes frightened or confused, it can attack with surprising speed on land or in the water.

Hh

Max length: 4.5 cm (1¾ in)

worldwide

Huntsman spider

This large spider is found in tropical and sub-tropical regions throughout the world. It does not spin a web, but relies on speed to catch prey, such as cockroaches, which it kills with a venomous bite. The venom is not dangerous to human beings. In some places this spider is a welcome visitor to people's homes, as it feeds on insects.

Fact

The huntsman spider is sometimes known as the housekeeping spider because it keeps houses clear of insect pests.

Max length: 1.5 m (5 ft)

Hyena

Although it looks like a wild dog, the spotted hyena is more closely related to cats than to wolves and foxes. The hyena lives in a large group known as a clan. Members of the clan cooperate while hunting to bring down large prey such as zebra. A hyena clan will also steal prey from lions and leopards.

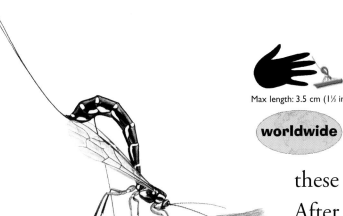

Max length: 3.5 cm (1⅓ in)

worldwide

Ichneumon wasp

There are many species of these insects, which are also called parasitic wasps. After mating, the females seek out the larvae of other insects, such as moths or butterfly caterpillars. Using a sting-like organ, the female wasp lays eggs inside the body of the caterpillar. When the wasp eggs hatch, the wasp larvae start to feed on the body of the caterpillar, eating it from the inside out.

Fact

In the deserts of the American Southwest, some ichneumon wasps specialise in laying their eggs inside the bodies of young tarantulas.

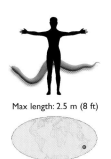

Max length: 2.5 m (8 ft)

Inland taipan

This rare Australian snake is one of the world's deadliest animals. The venom that the inland taipan uses to kill its prey is extremely strong. The venom gland in the snake's head contains enough poison to kill 100 human beings, and a single bite delivers enough venom to kill at least five.

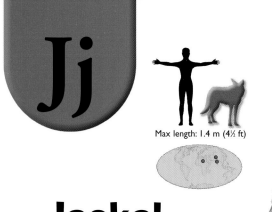

Jj

Max length: 1.4 m (4½ ft)

Jackal, golden

The golden jackal is closely related to wolves and foxes. It is widespread in North Africa, the Middle East and India. The golden jackal usually lives in a family group of two adults and their young, but it sometimes forms packs of up to 25 animals. This predator hunts small prey, such as rodents and lizards, but does not attack large animals.

Fact

Some killer whale pods are permanent residents in a particular patch of sea, while others regularly migrate across the oceans.

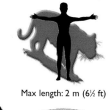

Max length: 2 m (6½ ft)

Jaguar

This large, powerful cat is found only in Central and South America. It prefers to live in wet, swampy forests where it hunts deer, wild pigs and other medium-sized mammals. The jaguar often crouches on a tree branch to ambush its prey by waterholes and river crossings.

Killer whale

Max length: 10 m (33 ft)

worldwide

The killer whale is the top ocean predator. This marine mammal is related to dolphins and shares their ability to find prey by using sound echoes. Killer whales, or orcas, live in family groups known as pods. They hunt a wide variety of sea animals including salmon, seals and other whales.

Kingfisher

Max length: 16 cm (6⅓ in)

worldwide

The kingfisher is found in all but the coldest parts of Europe and Asia. It builds its nest at the end of a burrow in the bank of a river or stream. The kingfisher hunts its prey and catches small fish in its beak by diving completely underwater from an overhanging branch.

Kite, black

Max length: 45 cm (17¾ in)

worldwide

The black kite is found in all parts of the world except North and South America and Antarctica. This medium-sized bird of prey is often a familiar sight as it soars over fields on the lookout for mice, lizards and young birds. In addition to hunting, the black kite has also become a scavenger on human rubbish dumps.

29

Kk

Komodo dragon

Max length: 3 m (10 ft)

The Komodo dragon is the largest and most dangerous lizard in the world. It is a type of flesh-eating monitor lizard that lives on four islands off the coast of Indonesia. A fully-grown Komodo is powerful enough to bring down prey the size of a horse, but it usually feeds on smaller animals. Its mouth contains more than 50 different types of bacteria. Several of these bacteria cause blood poisoning and death.

Krait, banded

Max length: 2.3 m (7½ ft)

The banded krait is a highly dangerous snake that lives in Southeast Asia. It is related to cobras but does not have their distinctive hood. The krait is active mainly at night, when it hunts small mammals and other reptiles. It can deliver deadly venom through its hollow front fangs.

Max length: 3.5 m (11½ ft)

Lion

Ll

The lion is the largest of the African big cats. It is the only cat that lives in groups of more than one adult. Groups of female lions and their cubs are called prides, and groups of male lions are called coalitions. Members of a group will cooperate while hunting large prey, such as buffalo. One lion waits in ambush while the others chase the prey towards the waiting ambusher.

Fact

Lions are found in only one place outside Africa – in the Gir forest of western India. These Indian lions are slightly smaller than their African relatives.

Lionfish

Max length: 40 cm (15¾ in)

This exotic-looking tropical fish has a deadly secret. Hidden among its feathery fins are long, sharp spines that can inject venom that is strong enough to kill a human being. Its vivid colour is a warning to would-be predators that if they try to eat the lionfish, they will get a mouthful of poison!

Ll

Max length: 3 mm (⅒ in)

worldwide

Louse

Like the flea, the louse is a wingless, parasitic insect that lives on the skin of mammals and birds. Some lice feed on fur or feathers, while others suck blood. In humans, head lice are unpleasant but not really dangerous. Human body lice, however, can transmit the deadly disease of typhus.

Max length: 1.4 m (4½ ft)

Lynx, Eurasian

The Eurasian lynx was once widespread in the forests of northern Europe and Asia, but it is now rare. Human activity has driven it into a few remote, mountainous regions. This medium-sized cat is the largest lynx. It prefers to hunt deer and wild goats, but will also catch rabbits and hares if it cannot find larger prey. It kills its prey by biting the animal's neck.

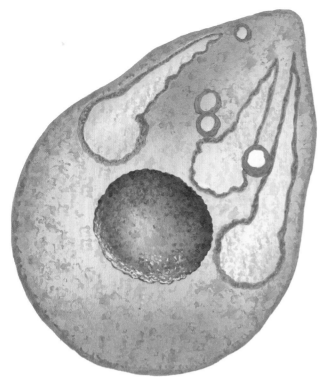

Length less than: 0.1 mm (⅟₂₅ in)

worldwide

Malaria parasite

This microscopically-small organism, which is called a plasmodium, lives in the digestive system of some mosquitoes and in human blood. In humans, the organism causes the disease of malaria, which every year kills millions of people in some tropical and sub-tropical regions around the world.

Fact
There are several different types of the disease malaria, which also affect apes, monkeys, rats and birds.

Max length: 5 cm (2 in)

Mantis shrimp

The mantis shrimp, which lives on coral reefs in the Indian Ocean, has a super-fast attack. Its front legs are powered by a kind of natural elastic, and they also have sharp claws at the end. Normally folded against the body, its front legs unfold at incredible speed to grab prey before it has a chance to escape.

Fact
The mantis shrimp gets its name because the quick unfolding of its front legs resembles the attack method of the praying mantis insect.

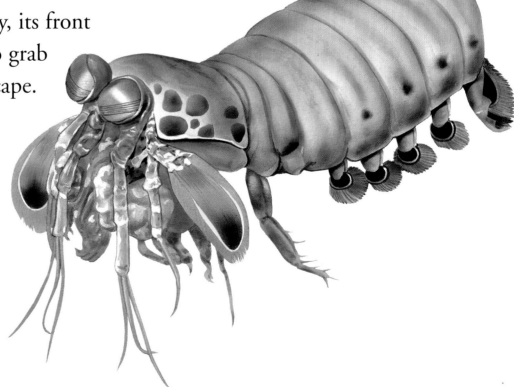

Mm

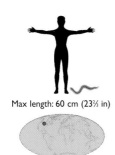
Max length: 60 cm (23⅗ in)

Massasagua

This small rattlesnake is found in damp, low-lying woodlands to the east of the Rocky Mountains in North America. It often lives in disused burrows in riverbanks, although it hunts mainly on land. The massasagua preys mostly on amphibians and small mammals, which it kills with a deadly, venomous bite.

Fact
Native Americans gave the massasagua its name. In the language of the Chippewa people, massasagua means 'Great River Mouth'.

Max length: 75 cm (29½ in)

Moonrat

The moonrat lives in the forests of Southeast Asia. It is related to hedgehogs and is mainly active at night, when it hunts for slugs and large insects on the forest floor. The moonrat is also an excellent swimmer and often dives into rivers in search of fish and other prey.

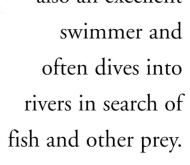

Max length: 7 mm (¼ in)

worldwide

Mosquito

The mosquito is a small flying, biting insect. It does not actually feed on blood, but females have to consume blood from a mammal in order to lay eggs. Some species of mosquito, found mainly in tropical regions, carry a parasite that causes the deadly disease of malaria in human beings. Other mosquito species can also transmit dangerous and unpleasant diseases, including yellow fever.

Max length: 1.8 m (6 ft)

Muskelunge

This large, freshwater fish is found in the rivers and lakes of eastern North America. Like its close relative the pike, the muskelunge is a fast-swimming predator. It has a large mouth with very sharp teeth. This creature will attack fish, amphibians, ducks and any small mammals that venture into the water.

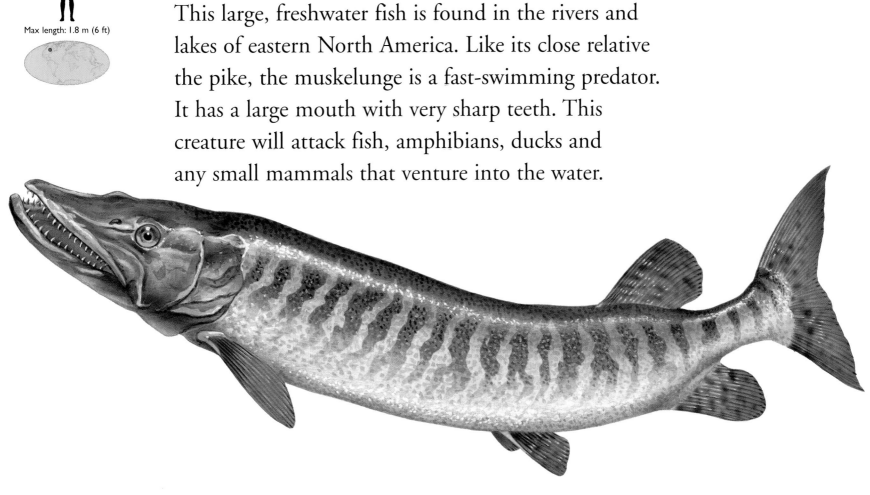

Nn

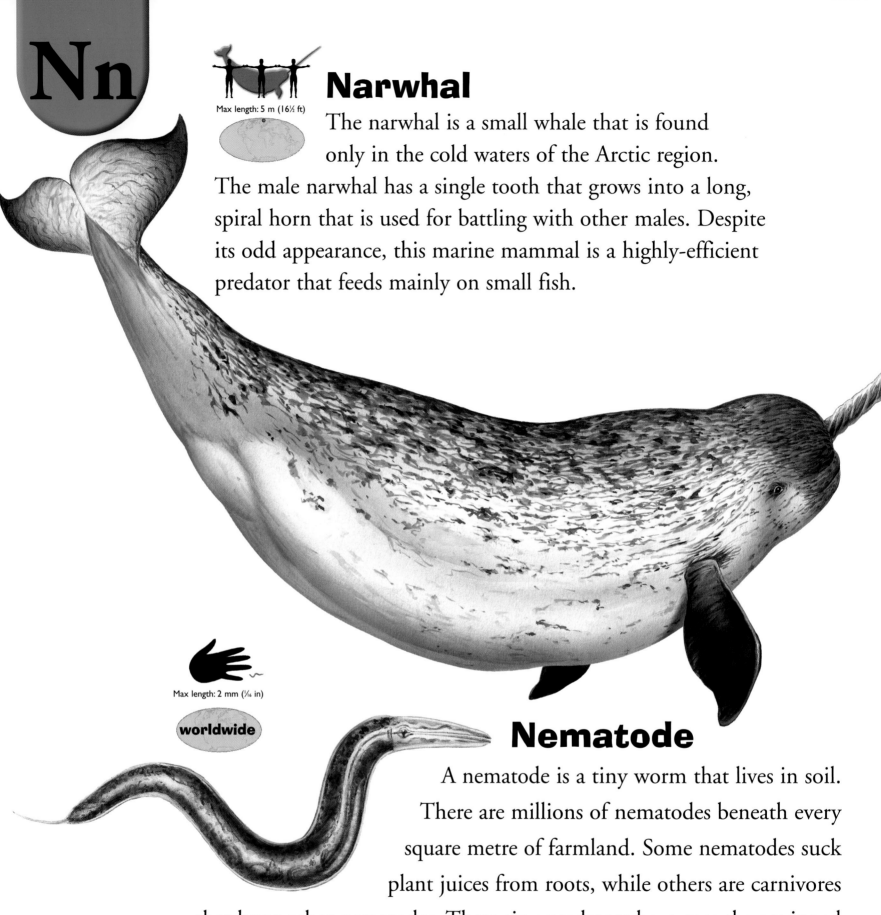

Max length: 5 m (16½ ft)

Narwhal

The narwhal is a small whale that is found only in the cold waters of the Arctic region. The male narwhal has a single tooth that grows into a long, spiral horn that is used for battling with other males. Despite its odd appearance, this marine mammal is a highly-efficient predator that feeds mainly on small fish.

Max length: 2 mm (⅟₁₆ in)

worldwide

Nematode

A nematode is a tiny worm that lives in soil. There are millions of nematodes beneath every square metre of farmland. Some nematodes suck plant juices from roots, while others are carnivores that hunt other nematodes. These tiny predators have mouths equipped with sharp, microscopically-small teeth to seize their prey. Some nematodes attack slugs by boring into their bodies.

Nile crocodile

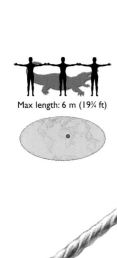

Max length: 6 m (19¾ ft)

The Nile crocodile is the most widespread of all the crocodiles and is found in lakes and rivers throughout Africa. This large reptile builds a nest on land but spends most of its time in water. Nile crocodiles mainly feed on fish, but they will also attack any birds or mammals that come within reach of their powerful jaws.

Fact

The Norway rat is also known as the brown rat, the barn rat, the wharf rat and the sewer rat.

Norway rat

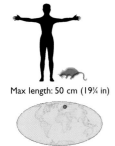

Max length: 50 cm (19¾ in)

This small rodent is responsible for millions of human deaths. Long ago, the Norway rat decided it preferred to feed around human settlements. Since then, it has spread around the world as a stowaway on ships. These rats contribute to the spread of disease. Worldwide, they consume millions of tonnes of human food and spoil much more with their droppings.

Oo

Max length: 12 cm (4¾ in)

Octopus, blue-ringed

The blue-ringed octopus lives in warm, shallow water in the Indian and Pacific oceans. The bright blue markings are a warning to other sea creatures that this little mollusc is deadly. Hidden among the tentacles is a sharp beak that can inflict a venomous bite. The venom is strong enough to kill a shark, a dolphin, or a human being.

Olive baboon

Max length: 1.3 m (4¼ ft)

This large monkey is found in Central Africa, where it lives in groups, known as troops, of up to 100 members. Although they are excellent tree climbers, olive baboons prefer to stay on the ground. The males in a troop will cooperate to hunt medium-sized mammals, such as gazelle fawns and zebra foals.

Oo

Osprey

Max length: 1.7 m (5½ ft)

worldwide

The osprey can be seen along coastlines in all parts of the world except Antarctica. This large bird of prey is often mistakenly called a fish eagle because fish are its favourite food. The osprey flies low over the ocean and uses its sharp talons to grab fish from just below the surface.

Fact
The feathers on an owl's wings and tail are specially designed to make no sound in flight, so that the bird can swoop down and catch its prey in total silence.

Owl, great horned

Max length: 60 cm (23⅗ in)

The great horned owl is found throughout North and South America. Like most owls, it hunts mainly at night. The great horned owl waits on a tree branch until it detects prey with its superb eyesight and hearing. It then glides down to grab its victim in its powerful talons.

39

Pp

Max length: 2.8 m (9 ft)

Panther

Panther is another name for the leopard, the most widespread of the big cats. Leopards are found from West Africa to Southeast Asia and in all kinds of environments, from deserts to mountain forests. The panther is a solitary animal that prefers to make surprise attacks by ambushing its prey rather than chasing after it.

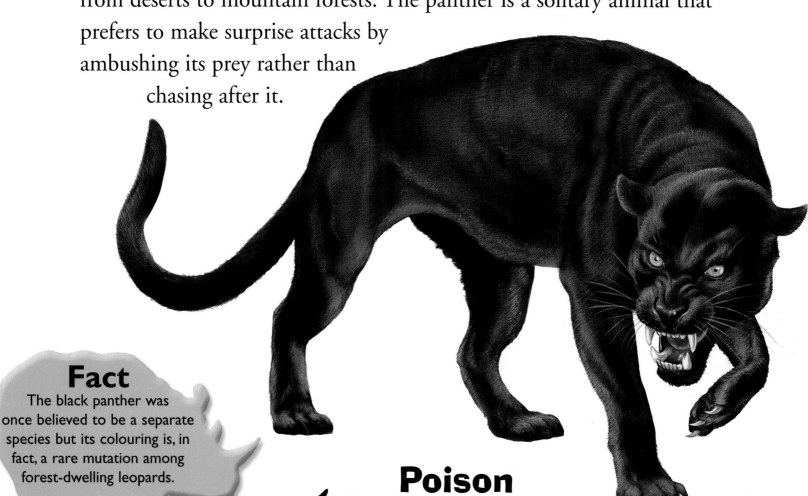

Fact
The black panther was once believed to be a separate species but its colouring is, in fact, a rare mutation among forest-dwelling leopards.

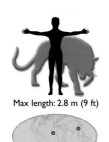

Max length: 4 cm (1½ in)

Poison dart frog

The poison dart frog lives in the tropical forests of Central and South America. Its bright colours warn predators that this amphibian is not good to eat. Special glands in the skin produce poisonous substances, which differ depending on the species. Native people use this substance on the tips of the darts they use for hunting.

Pp

Polar bear

Max length: 3.5 m (11½ ft)

The polar bear is the largest meat-eating animal that lives on land. It is a formidable predator. Kept warm by its thick fur, the polar bear inhabits the icy landscapes around the North Pole. It mainly hunts seals, and has enough strength to break through the ice in order to reach a seal in the water below.

Pond skater

Max length: 18 mm (¾ in)

worldwide

A pond skater is a small insect predator that lives on the surface of the water. It feeds on tiny flying insects, such as mosquitoes. The pond skater detects prey by feeling the vibrations on the water when an insect falls on to the surface. It then moves rapidly across the water's surface on its long legs. It does not break the surface tension that 'holds' the surface in place. Its short front legs hold the prey while it sucks the fluids out of the insect.

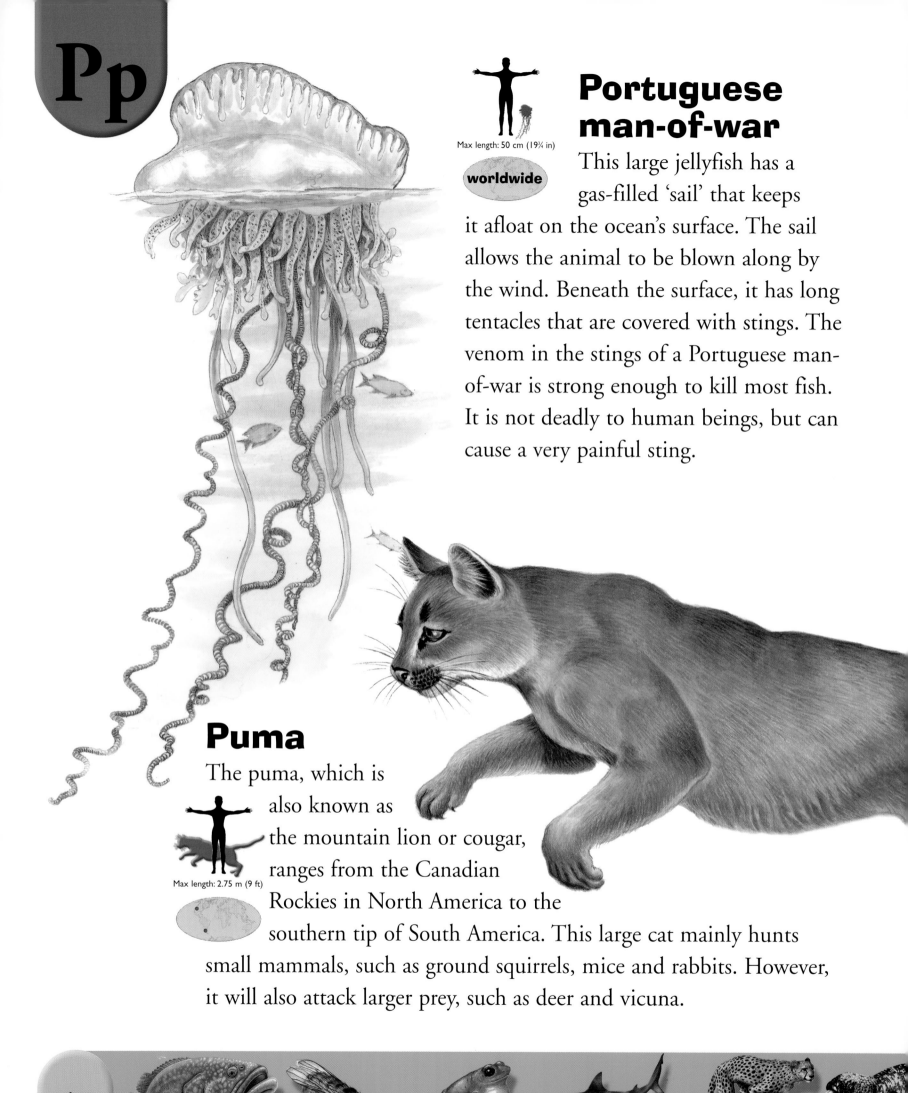

Pp

Portuguese man-of-war

Max length: 50 cm (19¾ in)

worldwide

This large jellyfish has a gas-filled 'sail' that keeps it afloat on the ocean's surface. The sail allows the animal to be blown along by the wind. Beneath the surface, it has long tentacles that are covered with stings. The venom in the stings of a Portuguese man-of-war is strong enough to kill most fish. It is not deadly to human beings, but can cause a very painful sting.

Puma

Max length: 2.75 m (9 ft)

The puma, which is also known as the mountain lion or cougar, ranges from the Canadian Rockies in North America to the southern tip of South America. This large cat mainly hunts small mammals, such as ground squirrels, mice and rabbits. However, it will also attack larger prey, such as deer and vicuna.

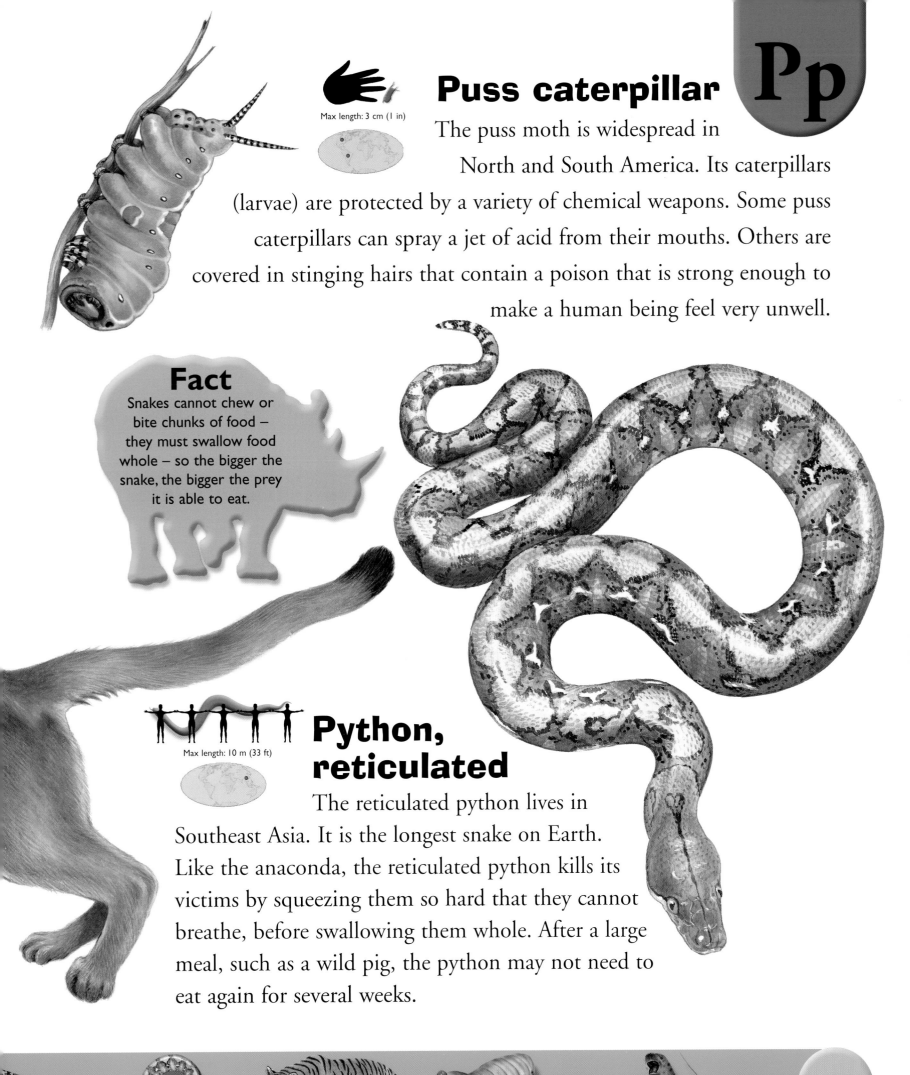

Max length: 3 cm (1 in)

Puss caterpillar

The puss moth is widespread in North and South America. Its caterpillars (larvae) are protected by a variety of chemical weapons. Some puss caterpillars can spray a jet of acid from their mouths. Others are covered in stinging hairs that contain a poison that is strong enough to make a human being feel very unwell.

Fact
Snakes cannot chew or bite chunks of food – they must swallow food whole – so the bigger the snake, the bigger the prey it is able to eat.

Max length: 10 m (33 ft)

Python, reticulated

The reticulated python lives in Southeast Asia. It is the longest snake on Earth. Like the anaconda, the reticulated python kills its victims by squeezing them so hard that they cannot breathe, before swallowing them whole. After a large meal, such as a wild pig, the python may not need to eat again for several weeks.

Qq

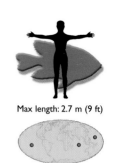

Max length: 2.7 m (9 ft)

Queensland grouper

This large fish is also known as the giant grouper. It is found throughout the warmer parts of the Indian and Pacific oceans. The Queensland grouper feeds mainly on lobsters and crabs. It crushes their shells in its powerful jaws. It will also eat sharks and rays and has been known to attack human beings.

Fact
Marsupials (pouched mammals) are found mainly in Australasia, but there are also some marsupial species in North and South America.

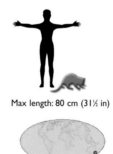

Max length: 80 cm (31½ in)

Quoll, eastern

The eastern quoll is a small, meat-eating marsupial that is now found only on the Australian island of Tasmania. It is sometimes called the native spotted cat, although it is more closely related to kangaroos than to cats. The eastern quoll is mainly active at night, when it hunts small mammals, birds and lizards.

Raccoon

Max length: 1.4 m (4½ ft)

The raccoon is found
in most parts of North
America, usually close to running
water. It lives in a communal den during
the day, but is solitary at night when it hunts.
The raccoon hunts crabs, crayfish and even fish,
and grabs its prey with the fingers of its front paws.

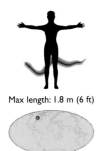

Max length: 1.8 m (6 ft)

Rattlesnake, timber

Rattlesnakes are found only in North and South
America. The timber rattlesnake lives in the
woodlands of the eastern United States.
The distinctive rattle is a warning to would-be
predators, but when hunting small prey, such as
mice and squirrels, the rattlesnake makes a silent
approach and delivers deadly venom with its front fangs.

Red fox

Max length: 1.4 m (4½ ft)

The most
widespread of
all wild dogs,
the red fox is found across
North America, Europe, Asia
and Australia. It does not
often form packs and usually
lives in small family groups.
The red fox is a solitary
hunter and preys mainly
on rabbits and hares.

Rr

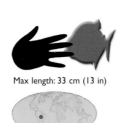

Max length: 33 cm (13 in)

Red piranha

This small predator lives in some South American rivers. Red piranhas often form groups of up to 100 fish. They normally feed on smaller prey, such as frogs and other fish, but a group of red piranhas will attack and kill much larger animals. They can attack prey as large as tapirs and bite off mouthfuls of flesh with their razor-sharp teeth.

Fact
The Amazon River has at least 1,500 named species of fish – five times more than in all European rivers put together.

Max length: 60 cm (23½ in)

Roadrunner, greater

The greater roadrunner is related to the cuckoo. It hunts lizards, snakes and small mammals in the deserts of the United States and Mexico. It can fly, but spends little time in the air. It rushes across the desert trying to scare its prey out into the open. It then kills its victims with a blow from its strong beak.

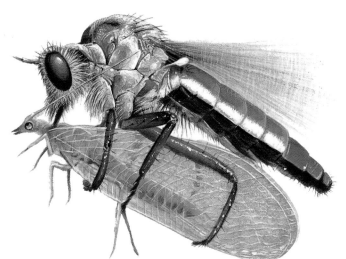

Max length: 5 cm (2 in)

worldwide

Robber fly

The robber fly, which is also known as the assassin fly, is the largest of all flies. It is a very efficient predator that catches other flying insects in midair. The robber fly grabs its prey with its elongated front legs and injects a substance that starts to dissolve the victim, making it easier to eat.

Fact

There are more than 80,000 species of fly. Some of them, such as the common housefly, spread disease and contaminate food with their droppings.

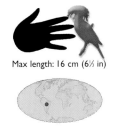

Max length: 16 cm (6⅓ in)

Royal flycatcher

This small bird lives in the tropical forests of Central and South America. Both males and females have a spectacular fan-shaped crest of feathers, which is normally kept folded flat. The royal flycatcher lives up to its name and feeds mainly on insects that it catches in midair.

Ss

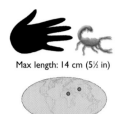

Max length: 14 cm (5½ in)

Scorpion, fat-tailed

The fat-tailed scorpion lives in the deserts of North Africa and the Middle East. It hides beneath rocks during the day and hunts insects and other small prey at night. The scorpion usually kills its victims with its powerful front claws. However, the sting in its tail can deliver a dose of venom strong enough to kill an adult human being.

Fact
Most people who are killed by scorpions are stung in the ankle or foot by a scorpion that they did not see.

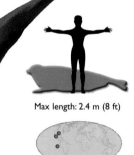

Max length: 2.4 m (8 ft)

Sea lion, California

The California sea lion is found close to the western coasts of the United States and Mexico, also around the Galapagos Islands. This marine mammal dives up to 75 metres (246 ft) below the surface in search of small fish and squid. Sea lions will also attack seabirds that are swimming at the surface.

Sea wasp

Max length: 20 cm (8 in)

Also known as the box jelly, this small jellyfish is found around the coasts of Australia at certain times of the year. Sea wasps often travel in large swarms, but the sting from just one of these animals is strong enough to kill a human being in just a few minutes.

Snow leopard

Max length: 2.3 m (7½ ft)

This rare mammal is found only in remote, mountainous regions of Central Asia. It has unusually thick fur to keep it warm and dry amid the ice and snow of its mountain home. The snow leopard is an extremely sure-footed hunter, able to chase wild goats across steep slopes that are covered with loose rocks and boulders.

Ss

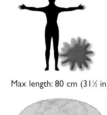

Max length: 1.2 m (4 ft)

Spitting cobra, red

The red spitting cobra, like other cobras, has hollow fangs that deliver deadly venom when it bites. This snake can also spray its venom into a victim's face from a distance of nearly 2 metres (6½ ft). If the venom comes into contact with the eyes, it causes instant blindness.

Max length: 80 cm (31½ in)

Starfish

The crown-of-thorns is an unusual starfish, protected by venomous spines. The venom is painful to human beings but deadly to smaller sea creatures. Most starfish feed on sea urchins and crabs, but the crown-of-thorns prefers smaller prey. It eats tiny coral animals that form the living surface of coral reefs.

Stingray

Max length: 2 m (6½ ft)

The stingray lives in shallow water around tropical coasts. It spends most of its time on the seabed, where it feeds on crabs and shellfish. About halfway along its tail is the sharp spine that gives the animal its name. As well as inflicting serious physical injury, this spine also delivers a dose of deadly venom.

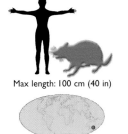

Max length: 24 cm (9½ in)

Tarantula

The Mombassa golden starburst tarantula is a large spider that is found in East Africa. It lives in an underground burrow and comes out at night to hunt small reptiles and mammals. Like other tarantulas, it has strong, downward-pointing fangs. It kills its victims by biting repeatedly rather than relying on venom.

Tasmanian devil

Max length: 100 cm (40 in)

This rare animal, which is found only on the Australian island of Tasmania, is the largest meat-eating marsupial. It has large jaws filled with strong, bone-crushing teeth. The Tasmanian devil is rarely seen during the day. It is mainly active at night when it hunts a variety of prey including insects, lizards and other marsupials.

Fact

There was once a marsupial carnivore called the thylacine or Tasmanian tiger, but it has not been seen since the 1930s and is probably now extinct.

Tt

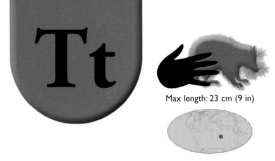

Max length: 23 cm (9 in)

Tenrec, lesser hedgehog

The lesser hedgehog tenrec is one of about 20 species of tenrec that live on the island of Madagascar. These small mammals specialise in eating beetles and other ground-living insects, which they catch with their sharp teeth. Some tenrecs, however, will also hunt larger prey, such as frogs and mice.

Fact
Among the tenrec's relatives are the solenodons – the only mammals that have a venomous bite.

Max length: 23 cm (9 in)

Thrush

The song thrush is well known as a songbird, but is much less known as a highly-efficient predator. The thrush searches the ground for insects and earthworms just below the surface, but snails are their favourite food. In order to get at the snail inside the shell, the thrush will smash the shell against a suitable stone.

Max length: 1 cm (½ in)

worldwide

Tick

The tick, which is related to the spider, is a small, bloodsucking parasite. It attaches itself to the skin of mammals, birds and reptiles. There are no ticks that specialise in feeding on human blood, but many ticks will take such a meal if they get the opportunity. Some of these can transmit deadly diseases, such as Lyme disease.

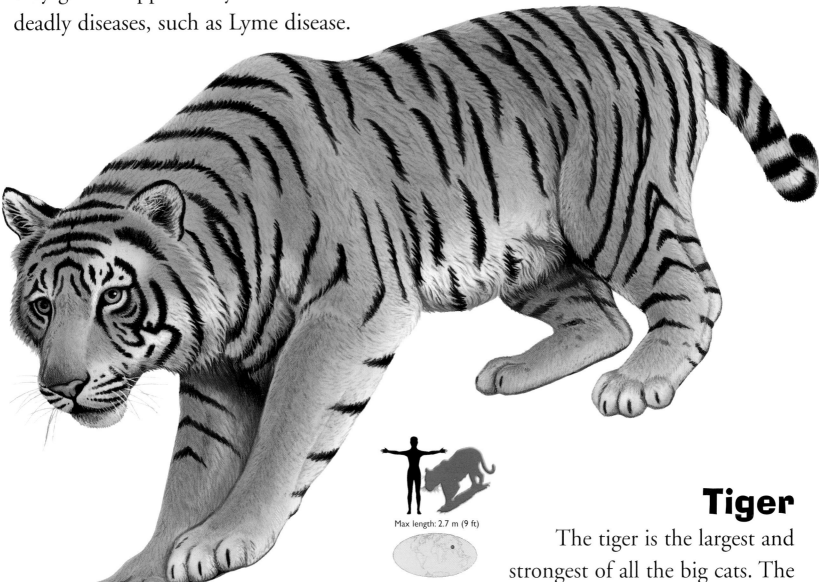

Max length: 2.7 m (9 ft)

Tiger

The tiger is the largest and strongest of all the big cats. The tiger was once widespread across southern Asia, but they are now found mainly in national parks and wildlife refuges. The tiger prefers to hunt medium-sized forest animals, such as deer. But if its usual prey is in short supply, a tiger will also attack and eat human beings.

Max length: 16 mm (⅔ in)

worldwide

Tiger beetle, green

The green tiger beetle is a ferocious insect predator. It can fly short distances, but always hunts on the ground. The green tiger beetle mainly feeds on slow-moving prey, such as caterpillars, which it grabs in its powerful jaws. It can also run at considerable speed when chasing after faster-moving insects.

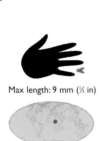

Max length: 9 mm (⅓ in)

Tsetse fly

This small, bloodsucking fly is found across much of central Africa. It feeds on the blood of mammals. The amount of blood each fly consumes is harmless, but its bite can be deadly. The tsetse fly transmits the disease known as sleeping sickness, which is much more dangerous than it sounds. In Africa, sleeping sickness kills thousands of people each year.

Fact
Tsetse flies have an even more devastating effect on cattle and horses than on human beings. The presence of these flies makes cattle ranching impossible in large areas of Africa.

Ungava seal

Max length: 1.8 m (6 ft)

The Ungava seal is an unusual variety of the common or harbour seal. It is found only in some freshwater lakes in northeastern Canada. Like other seals, it is an agile predator that dives beneath the surface to chase after fish. The Ungava seal can stay underwater for up to six or seven minutes at a time.

Fact
Seals are brilliant swimmers. Some can stay underwater for more than an hour.

Vanga, sickle-billed

Max length: 12.7 cm (5 in)

The sickle-billed vanga is a small bird that feeds on insects and small reptiles in the thorny forests on the island of Madagascar. The long, curved beak is perfectly shaped for grabbing prey that is hiding among the thorns. Other species of vanga on the island have differently-shaped beaks that are appropriate for catching prey in different environments.

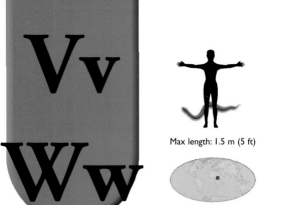

Viper, bush

Max length: 1.5 m (5 ft)

The bush viper is found in the tropical forests of central Africa. It is an ambush predator that feeds on frogs, lizards and small mammals. This snake often hangs from a branch by its tail and waits for suitable prey to pass underneath. The bush viper kills its victims with venom injected by its hollow front fangs.

Fact
The young vipers have a light-coloured tail tip that they use as a lure to encourage prey to come close by.

Water scorpion

Max length: 2 cm (¾ in)

worldwide

This small animal is an insect, not a scorpion. It lives in freshwater ponds and lakes, where it feeds on tadpoles and small fish. The water scorpion catches its prey with its powerful front legs. The long 'sting' at the end of its abdomen is actually a breathing tube for use when the insect is underwater.

Max length: 6 cm (2⅓ in)

worldwide

Whelk

The whelk is a type of marine snail. There are hundreds of species and they are found in all but the coldest waters. The whelk is a seabed predator, which feeds on other shellfish, especially oysters and mussels. It has a long, sharp snout that it uses to bore a hole into the victim's shell.

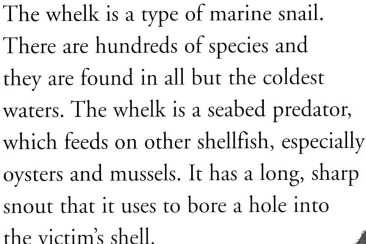

Max length: 2 m (6½ ft)

Wolf, grey

The grey wolf is the largest of the wild dogs and has a fearsome reputation as a predator. It lives and hunts in packs of about 8–12 animals. By working together, the pack can bring down prey as big as a moose or elk. Grey wolves were once numerous in North America and northern Asia, but they are now quite rare.

Fact

Although all grey wolves belong to the same species, they vary according to their location – those in Alaska are bigger and paler in colour than those in Scandinavia.

Ww
Xx

Max length: 1.25 m (4 ft)

Max length: 4.5 m (14¾ ft)

worldwide

Wolverine

The wolverine is a fierce, flesh-eating relative of the badger, which lives in cold, northern regions. It is a highly-effective predator that can chase small prey, such as rabbits, but will also ambush animals as large as elk. The wolverine, which is also known as the glutton, will often bury part of its prey in snow and then return to finish its meal some time later.

Xiphias gladius

Xiphias gladius is the scientific name for the swordfish (*gladius* means 'sword'). It is one of the biggest predatory fish and is larger and faster than most sharks. The swordfish feeds on squid and small fish. It makes a high-speed attack and uses its sword to slash its prey into pieces that can be easily swallowed.

Yellow-winged bat

Max length: 8 cm (3 in)

The yellow-winged bat is found across central Africa. During the day, it roosts in thorn trees but, at night, it takes to the air to hunt flying insects. Like many other bats it has poor eyesight and uses echolocation – high-pitched sound waves – to detect its prey in complete darkness.

Fact
Bats that use echolocation usually have strangely-shaped noses to focus their high-pitched squeaks.

Zorro, Sechuran

Max length: 1.3 m (4¼ ft)

The Sechuran zorro is a small, South American fox that lives in the coastal deserts of Peru. It hunts a wide range of small prey, such as beetles, lizards and mice. The Sechuran zorro is found in areas that have no streams or pools, so it probably survives by licking up dew from rocks and vegetation.

Glossary

Amphibian An air-breathing animal with a backbone that lays its eggs in freshwater. Frogs and toads are the most commonly encountered types of amphibian.

Bacteria Single-celled organisms – some of which can cause disease.

Bat One of about 1,000 species of flying mammals, which are mainly active at night.

Bird A warm-blooded animal with a backbone and a feather-covered body. A bird lays hard-shelled eggs.

Carnivore An animal that eats the freshly-killed bodies of other animals.

Caterpillar The larva (juvenile form) of a moth or butterfly.

Cold-blooded Describes any animal that relies on its environment to maintain its body temperature. Reptiles, amphibians and fish are the main groups of cold-blooded animals, along with insects, spiders, molluscs and all other non-backboned animals.

Disease Any malfunction of a plant or animal body. An infectious disease is one that can be passed from one individual to another.

Eel One of a group of unusual fish that have long, slender bodies and usually a single fin.

Fang A sharp, hollow tooth designed to inject venom.

Food chain An arrangement of plants and animals according to their feeding habits. For example, a hawk eats sparrows, which eat caterpillars, which eat the leaves on an apple tree.

Food web A diagram showing all the food chains in a particular place.

Freshwater Rainwater, river water and the water in most lakes is called freshwater because it contains no salt.

Gland A body part that produces substances that are used elsewhere.

Glossary

Herbivore An animal that feeds on plants.

Host An animal that is carrying external or internal parasites.

Insect A small, six-legged animal that does not have a backbone and often has wings.

Jaws The hinged bones of the mouth, which hold the teeth.

Larva (larvae is plural) The juvenile or young form of an insect, which changes its appearance when it becomes an adult.

Lizard One of a large group of generally small- to medium-sized, land-living reptiles.

Lyme disease A disease found in deer that can be passed to human beings by ticks.

Malaria A disease caused by microscopic organisms that are passed to humans by mosquito bites.

Mammal A warm-blooded animal with a backbone that produces live-born young. Most mammals are covered with hair and live on land. There are a few marine mammals such as seals, whales and dolphins.

Marine Describes anything to do with the seas and oceans.

Marsupial One of a group of mammals that carry and care for their young in a special pouch on the female body.

Mollusc One of a group of soft-bodied animals that do not have bones. Some molluscs, such as snails, make hard, protective shells for themselves. Another group of molluscs that includes octopus and squid, have no external shell and are equipped with long, grasping tentacles.

Glossary

Organ A body part that has a specific purpose. For example, the eye is an organ for seeing.

Parasite An animal that lives in or on the body of another animal (called the host) and which feeds on the host.

Poison Any substance that is harmful to living things.

Predator An animal that hunts and eats other animals.

Prey An animal that is hunted and eaten by others.

Reptile A cold-blooded animal with a backbone, which breathes air and produces live young, hard-shelled eggs, or eggs with leathery shells. Crocodiles, lizards, turtles, tortoises and snakes are all reptiles.

Rodent One of a group of small mammals that includes rats, mice and squirrels, but not rabbits and hares.

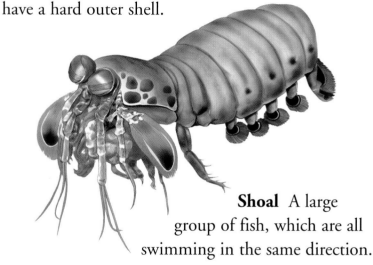

Scales Small, disc-like plates that protect the skin of snakes, lizards and most fish.

Scavenger An animal that feeds on the bodies of animals that are already dead.

Shellfish A non-scientific term for sea creatures, such as crabs, shrimps and some molluscs, that have a hard outer shell.

Shoal A large group of fish, which are all swimming in the same direction.

Snake One of a large group of legless reptiles.

Species The particular scientific group to which an individual animal (or plant) belongs. Each species is a unique design and has a two-part scientific name. Members of the same species all share the same characteristics and differ only slightly in colour or size.